Girlfriends' GET-TOGETHER Craft Book

KATHY ROSS

ILLUSTRATED BY NICOLE in den BOSCH

M Millbrook Press/Minneapolis

For my Thursday night dinner group—
a great girlfriends' get-together
—KR

Millbrook Press, Inc.
A division of Lerner Publishing Group
241 First Avenue North
Minneapolis, MN 55401 U.S.A.

Website address: www.lernerbooks.com

Library of Congress Cataloging-in-Publication Data

Ross, Kathy (Katharine Reynolds), 1948–
    The girlfriends' get-together craft book / Kathy Ross ; illustrated by Nicole in den Bosch.
        p. cm. — (Girl crafts)
    Summary: Provides step-by-step directions for twenty-two crafts designed for those who are interested in fashion, decor, dolls, and jewelry.
    ISBN-13: 978-0-7613-3408-8 (lib. bdg. : alk. paper)
    ISBN-10: 0-7613-3408-4 (lib. bdg. : alk. paper)
    1. Handicraft for girls—Juvenile literature. 2. Sleepovers—Planning—Juvenile literature.
        I. Bosch, Nicole in den. II. Title. III. Series.
    TT171.R69 2007
    745.5—dc22   2005035668

Manufactured in the United States of America
1 2 3 4 5 6 — JR — 12 11 10 09 08 07

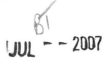

Contents

Make this project even more fun by asking everyone coming to your party to bring some colorful fabric to share.

Room Pennants

Here is what you need:

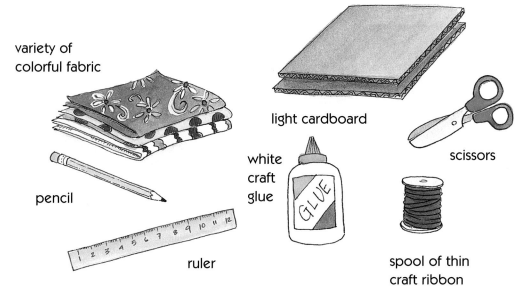

variety of colorful fabric

pencil

ruler

light cardboard

white craft glue

scissors

spool of thin craft ribbon

Here is what you do:

1. Make a pattern for the pennant on the light cardboard. A triangle with a 9-inch (23-cm) base and 12-inch (30-cm) sides is a good size for each pennant. Cut the pennant pattern out.

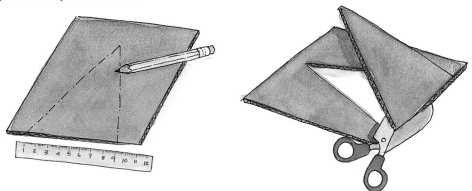

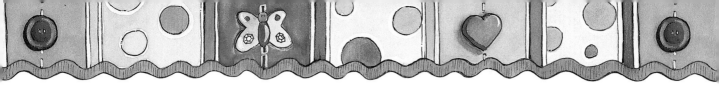

2. Fold over a piece of fabric. Place the base of the triangle pattern on the fold of the fabric so that the pennant will have the fabric print on the front and the back.

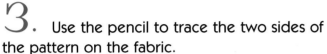

3. Use the pencil to trace the two sides of the pattern on the fabric.

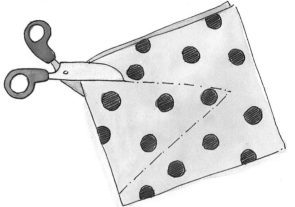

4. Cut out the fabric pennant.

5. Make several pennants in different types of fabric.

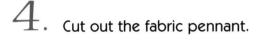

(continued on next page)

6. Unwind the spool of ribbon. Fold one end over and knot it to form a loop for hanging.

7. Hang the pennants over the ribbon, spacing them about 6 inches (15 cm) apart. You string of pennants should be long enough to reach across the area where you will hang it. Secure each pennant with a couple of dots of glue between the front and back near the point of the pennant. Use just a little glue so that it does not soak through the fabric and stain the pennants.

8. If you do not use all the ribbon, trim off the extra before tying the second end into a loop for hanging.

Be creative in finding fabric to use for making pennants. Discarded clothing, curtains, and tablecloths are all good sources of pretty fabric.

Have everyone bring their flip-flops
to embellish using this summer craft idea.

Fancy Flip-Flops

Here is what you need:

variety of colorful, narrow
ribbons or strips of fabric

pair of flip-flops

white craft glue

scissors

ruler

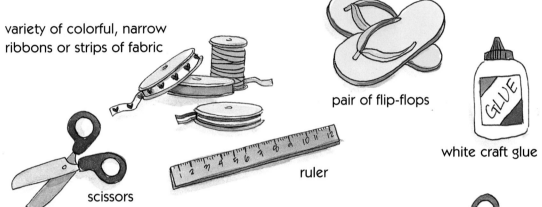

Here is what you do:

1. Cut about twenty 6-inch (15-cm) pieces
of ribbon or 1-inch (2.5-cm) wide fabric strips
for each flip-flop.

2. Fold each strip in half. Hold the folded ribbon
under the foot band on the flip-flop. Then bring the
ribbon ends up around the band and through the
fold. Pull the ends tight. Place a dab of glue under
the fold to secure it.

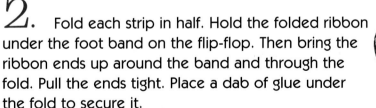

3. Cover the bands
on both flip-flops with
ribbon or fabric strips.

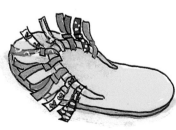

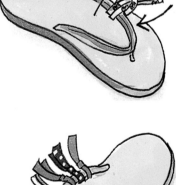

**For waterproof flip-flops, try making strips from
plastic bags or a disposable plastic tablecloth.**

Collect discarded pierced earrings and beads,
and design your own fancy ladies!

Junk Jewelry Picture Board

Here is what you need:

five 8- by 12-inch (20- by 30-cm) pieces of craft foam

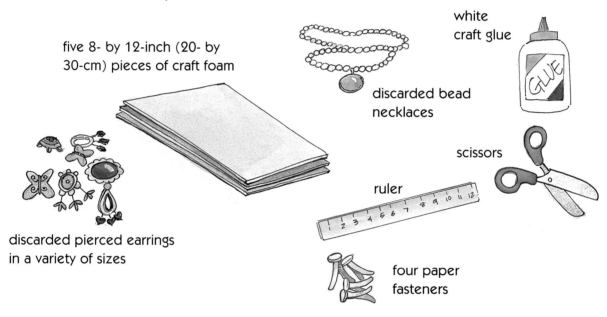

discarded pierced earrings in a variety of sizes

discarded bead necklaces

white craft glue

ruler

scissors

four paper fasteners

Here is what you do:

1. Create a picture board by stacking the five pieces of craft foam and securing them at the four corners with the paper fasteners.

2. Select some large earrings to use as heads for the ladies.

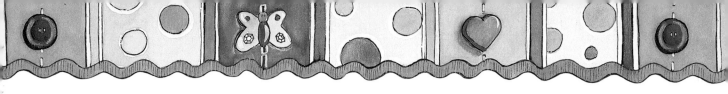

3. Cut 1-inch (2.5-cm) strips of beads from the discarded necklaces to glue on the heads for smiles. Glue on single beads for noses and eyes. (If you can't find beads that are small enough, you can use seed beads.)

4. Stick the head into the foam picture board.

5. Add small earrings on each side of the head for earrings for the fancy lady. Use other earrings for the hat and body. Dangling earrings are perfect for the arms and legs. Use another earring for a purse.

More earrings mean more fun—so ask your girlfriends to bring as many discarded earrings as they can.

Your guests can hunt for their own materials for this project . . . outdoors!

Sticks Photo Display Easel

Here is what you need:

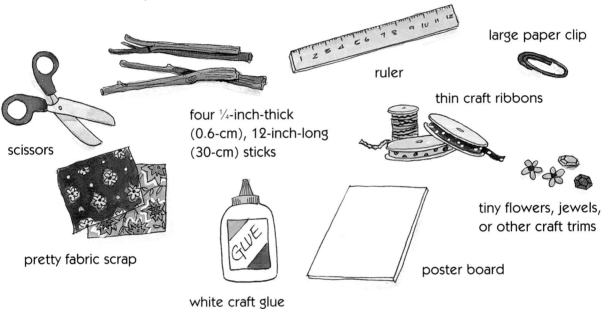

scissors

four ¼-inch-thick (0.6-cm), 12-inch-long (30-cm) sticks

ruler

large paper clip

thin craft ribbons

pretty fabric scrap

white craft glue

poster board

tiny flowers, jewels, or other craft trims

Here is what you do:

1. Cut a 24-inch (60-cm) length of thin ribbon.

2. Tie three of the sticks together at the top by first wrapping the ribbon around them separately and then wrapping them together. Tie the ends into a knot.

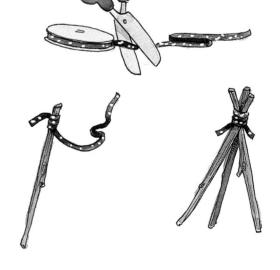

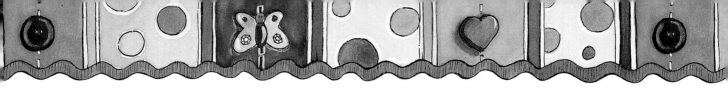

3. Arrange the bottoms of the three sticks like an easel to make the sticks stand.

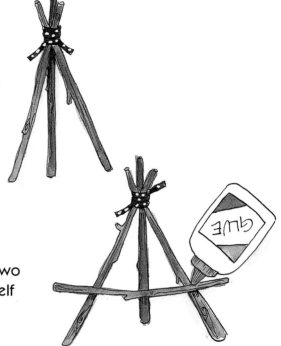

4. Glue the last stick across the center of the two front sticks to create a shelf for the easel.

5. Secure the contact points by wrapping ribbon around the sticks and tying the ends in a bow.

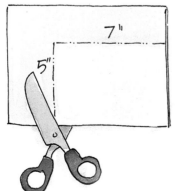

7"

5"

6. Cut a 5- by 7-inch (13- by 18-cm) piece of poster board.

(continued on next page)

7. Cover the poster board with the pretty fabric scrap.

8. Slip the paper clip over the bottom center of the poster board to use as a holder for a picture or photo.

9. Glue the poster board to the front of the easel.

10. Glue the flowers, jewels, and trims to the top of the poster board and to the easel for decoration.

You might want to ask someone to take a digital camera picture of you and your friends at the party, and print a copy for each person to display on her own easel.

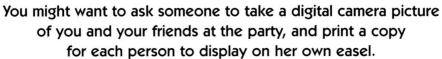

This adorable project is so easy!

Poodle Pin

Here is what you need:

poodle appliqué

white craft glue

thin ribbon or trim

scissors

pin-back

package of craft pearls

Here is what you do:

1. Highlight the parts of the poodle's coat that are puffy by gluing pearls over the area.

2. Use the thin ribbon or trim to make a collar or neck bow for the poodle. Glue it in place. Let it dry.

3. Glue the pin-back on the back of the poodle.

How many ways can you and your friends think of to wear the pin? It would look just as wonderful on a purse or skirt as on a collar!

Delightful Doorknob Decor

Here is what you need:

discarded sock
with stretchy cuff

pony beads and/or
jingle bells

fifteen 12-inch (30-cm) pieces
of ribbon and/or 1-inch
(2.5-cm) wide fabric strips

white craft glue

scissors

Here is what you do:

1. Cut the cuff off the sock.

2. Roll the cuff to create a band
that will slip over a doorknob.

3. Tie each ribbon or fabric strip, equally spaced, around the cuff so that the ends of each strip are of equal length.

4. Slip a pony bead or jingle bell partway up some of the ribbons or fabric strips.

5. Secure with a dab of glue or by knotting the ribbon or fabric strip below the bead or bell. Note: If you put a jingle bell or two on the ribbons, you will always know when someone is coming into your room.

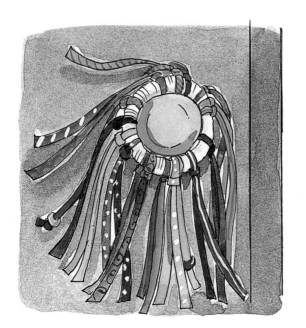

Try choosing materials in different color combinations to use at different times of the year.

Make an ordinary tissue box extraordinary.

Extremely Elegant Tissue Box

Here is what you need:

scissors

square box
of tissues

white craft glue

thin ribbon

artificial flowers

seed beads

old paper
doll lady

Here is what you do:

1. Cut across the paper doll at the waist to remove the bottom half.

2. Turn the tissue box on one side so that the tissue will hang down.

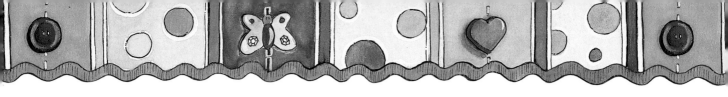

3. Glue the top half of the paper doll to the top center of the box so that the tissue hanging down becomes a skirt for the doll.

4. Glue a band of seed beads across the neck of the doll for a necklace.

5. Glue a ribbon bow or flowers to the hair of the doll.

6. Glue ribbons and strings of seed beads to the waist of the doll so that they hang down over the skirt.

7. Glue a bouquet of artificial flowers in the hand of the paper doll.

This is just one idea for decorating the paper doll, but I'm sure you and your girlfriends will have lots of good ideas of your own.

Have each guest bring a fashion doll to use
as a model for this project.

Beautiful Bonnet

Here is what you need:

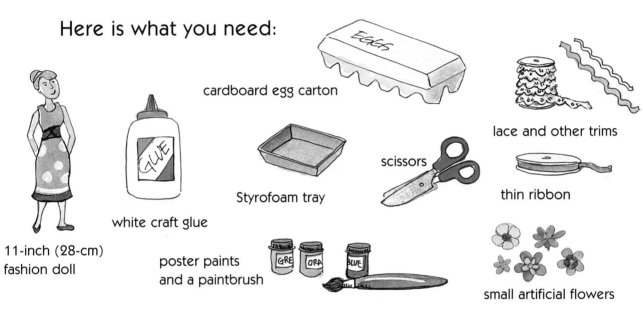

cardboard egg carton

lace and other trims

Styrofoam tray

scissors

thin ribbon

white craft glue

11-inch (28-cm)
fashion doll

poster paints
and a paintbrush

small artificial flowers

Here is what you do:

1. Cut one cup from the cardboard egg carton.

2. Trim away one side of the cup until it fits the back of the doll's head like a bonnet.

3. Working on the Styrofoam tray, paint the cup inside and out. Let it dry completely on the tray.

4. Glue a lace ruffle around the inner front brim of the bonnet.

5. Cut a 12-inch (30-cm) piece of thin ribbon.

6. Glue the ribbon around the outer brim of the bonnet so that the two ends hang down on each side to form the ties for the bonnet.

7. Glue additional trim around the edge of the outer brim of the bonnet, covering the thin ribbon so that only the ties hanging down still show.

8. Glue a small flower on each side of the hat.

For dolls with larger heads, use disposable plastic cups or containers that just fit over the head of the doll.

Give a plain T-shirt pizzazz with this idea!

Trendy T-Shirt

Here is what you need:

T-shirt

white craft glue

variety of different thin ribbons

scissors

Here is what you do:

1. Choose a square area of a T-shirt that you would like to decorate. If there is a stain or small hole on the shirt, this might be a good area to use, as the ribbon weaving will help to hide the damage.

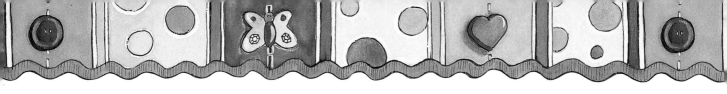

2. Fold in half only the front area of the shirt. Cut six 1-inch (2.5-cm) slits about ¼- to ½-inch (1-cm) apart. When the area is unfolded, there will be six 2-inch (5-cm) slits in the shirt.

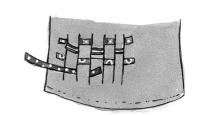

3. Cut several 6-inch (15-cm) lengths of different ribbons.

4. Weave the ribbon strips in and out of the slits in the T-shirt.

5. Trim the ends of the ribbon so that they are even on each side.

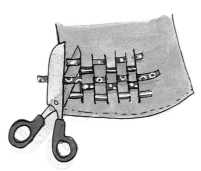

6. You can secure the ribbons with glue or leave them unglued so you can remove them for washing or to change the ribbon design.

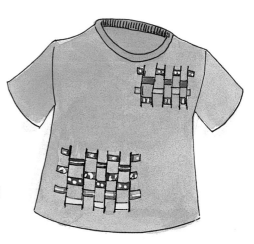

7. If you want more than one ribbon square on the shirt, choose another area and repeat the process. You can vary the number and length of the cuts to make smaller or larger patches of woven ribbon.

You might want to add a small bead or two to the ends of some of the ribbons.

Turn an old stuffed animal into a place to stash your pj's!

Pajama Bag Friend

Here is what you need:

felt scraps

ribbon

sticky-back
Velcro strip

white craft glue

scissors

two large
pom-poms

large, old
stuffed animal

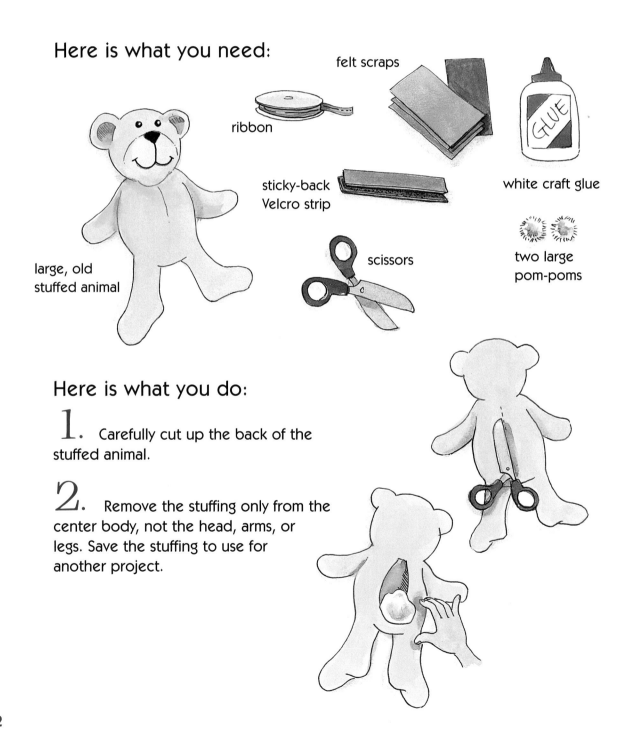

Here is what you do:

1. Carefully cut up the back of the
stuffed animal.

2. Remove the stuffing only from the
center body, not the head, arms, or
legs. Save the stuffing to use for
another project.

3. Cut a length of Velcro strip as long as the cut in the back of the stuffed animal.

4. Stick the two pieces of Velcro together. Press one sticky side to the right side of the edge of the cut in the fabric of the stuffed animal.

5. Fold in about 1 inch (2.5 cm) on the left side of the cut fabric. Stick the inner folded fabric to the sticky top of the Velcro strip. The Velcro strip will allow you to open and close the back of the stuffed animal.

6. Add details to the stuffed animal such as heart cheeks and flowers using pieces of glued-on cut felt.

7. Tie ribbons around the neck and ears.

8. Glue a large pom-pom to the top of each foot to look like slippers.

This is a great way to use a damaged stuffed animal. The felt and ribbon decorations can be used to hide holes and stains.

You and your girlfriends will want to make several
of these easy and elegant corsages.

Decorative Flower Corsage

Here is what you need:

artificial flowers

scissors

variety of thin ribbon,
eyelash thread, trims

pipe cleaner

fancy shank buttons

safety pin

white craft glue

ruler

Here is what you do:

1. Pull the center out of a flower, and separate the layers of petals. You can use petals from different flowers to create the new flower.

2. Choose three or four circles of petals to layer together. When you're happy with the arrangement, use small dabs of flue to hold the petals in place.

3.
Cut a 3-inch (8-cm) piece of the pipe cleaner.

4.
Thread the piece of pipe cleaner through the back of a button. Then thread the two ends down through the hole in the center of the stacked flower petals.

5.
Cut two 12-inch-long (30-cm) pieces of trim or ribbon. Tie the pieces around one of the pipe cleaner ends at the back of the flower so that the ends hang down from the bottom of the flower.

6.
Slide a closed safety pin on the other pipe cleaner end. Then twist the two ends together to secure the flower, ribbons, and safety pin.

7.
Fold the ends of the pipe cleaner back so they will not poke the wearer of the flower.

This versatile flower can be used to decorate your room or yourself!

Remember those magnetic letters you and your girlfriends used to play with?

My Message Board

Here is what you need:

magnetic letters

tiny flowers, jewels, charms, beads, pom-poms, other collage materials

ribbon

scissors

white craft glue

old metal cookie sheet, pizza pan, or lid from a tin container

Here is what you do:

1. Select the letters for your name plus a short message, such as "DO THIS," if the tin is large enough.

2. Decorate each letter by gluing on a tiny flower, bead, jewel, or other collage item. They can all match or be different.

3. Cut a piece of ribbon long enough to go all the way around the outside of the tin board and enough extra to tie the ends together for a hanger for the board. Secure the ribbon to the bottom and the sides of the board with glue.

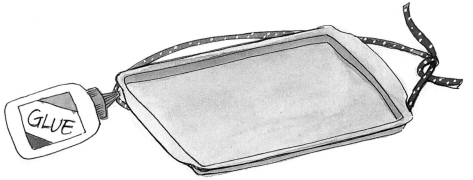

4. Decorate the outer rim of the metal board with small bows, flowers, or other collage materials.

Use the decorated letters to hang up your notes and reminders.

Dresser knobs form the noses for this cute craft.

Knob-Nose Buddies

Here is what you need:

yarn bits

package of round, cotton makeup pads

small pom-poms, beads, jewels, flowers, and other collage materials

scissors

wiggle eyes

thin craft ribbon

white craft glue

fat markers

Here is what you do:

1. Cut an X shape in the center of a round cotton pad that is just large enough to allow it to slip over a knob on your dresser. It is easiest to cut the slits in the center by folding the round in half and cutting on the fold, then reopening it.

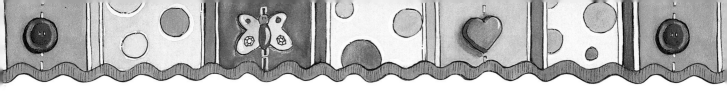

2. Decide what character face you are going to make with the cotton pad, remembering that the dresser knob will become the nose when you slip the cotton round over the knob.

3. If you need to add extra pieces for an animal, such as a rabbit or bear, cut the ears from a second cotton pad and glue them in place on the face.

4. Use collage materials to create the face. Make a different character for each knob on the dresser.

Try making different sets of characters for different seasons of the year. For example, you could make a set of pumpkins for October or cut the rounds into hearts for February. The rounds can be colored gently with the side of a fat marker.

With this project stashed in a purse or backpack, it will be easy for you and your girlfriends to pass notes!

Purse Pad

Here is what you need:

scissors

ruler

white craft glue

thin craft ribbon

white copy paper

discarded compact, empty and cleaned

pretty fabric scrap

stapler and staples

Here is what you do:

1. To make a pattern, press a small piece of the copy paper inside the compact where the makeup was.

2. Cut out the pattern. Use the pattern to cut a stack of about ten sheets of paper to fit in the compact.

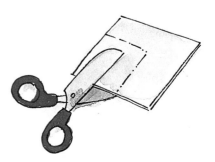

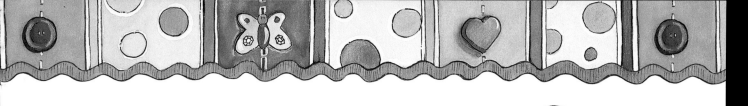

3. Staple the sheets together at the top and place them in the compact. Save the pattern to make refills for the purse pad.

4. Cut a 12-inch (30-cm) length of the ribbon.

5. Glue the center of the ribbon to the center of the bottom of the compact. The ribbon ends should be long enough so that they stick out on each side and can be tied together at the top of the compact.

6. Cut two simple 1-inch (2.5-cm) shapes from the fabric.

7. Glue one shape to the bottom of the compact over the center of the ribbon.

8. Glue the second shape to the top of the compact.

9. Tie the ribbon ends in a bow at the top of the compact.

You might want to use photos or pictures cut from greeting cards on the compact instead of the fabric shapes.

Have some creative fun with old paper dolls.

Paper Doll Booklet

Here is what you need:

white construction paper

white craft glue

tiny trims, ribbons, flowers, sequins, and other collage materials

markers

scissors

paper doll

ruler

four or more paper doll outfits

Here is what you do:

1. Make a booklet from the white paper with each page as long as the paper doll dresses. You can make three double pages by folding the pages in half at the center to make two pages from each sheet.

2. Fold the pages together to close the booklet. Cut two small triangles on the fold of the papers.

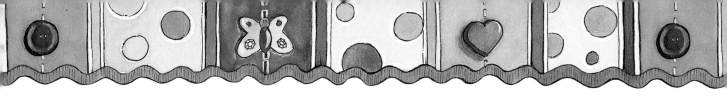

3. Open the booklet, cut a 12-inch (30-cm) length of the ribbon, thread an end of the ribbon through each hole at the center. Close the booklet and tie the ends of the ribbon together in a bow on the outside fold.

4. Glue the paper doll to the back page of the book so that the head is just above the pages of the booklet. If the dresses for the doll are short, the legs will stick out from the bottom of the booklet. If the dresses are long, the entire body will be glued to the back page of the book.

5. Cut the tabs from the dresses.

6. Glue a dress on each page of the book for the doll. Use the markers to add missing arms and neck area if needed.

7. Decorate the dresses by gluing on the collage materials.

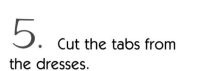

You and your girlfriends can also draw your own dresses on some or all of the pages of the booklet. The hand-drawn outfits can be colored or covered with printed paper or fabric, then decorated with collage items.

Turn colorful round balloons into pretty flowers.

Balloon Blossoms

Here is what you need:

green, yellow, and orange pipe cleaners

12-inch (30-cm) round balloons in a variety of colors

2½-inch (6.5-cm) clay flowerpot or other small container

white craft glue

scissors

ruler

thin craft ribbons

1-inch (2.5-cm) Styrofoam ball

Here is what you do:

1. Cut a 2-inch (5-cm) piece of yellow or orange pipe cleaner. Fold the piece in half to make the stamen for the flower.

2. Cut a 6-inch (15-cm) piece of the green pipe cleaner.

3. Fold one end of the green pipe cleaner over the fold of the stamen to attach it to the stamen to form the stem for the flower.

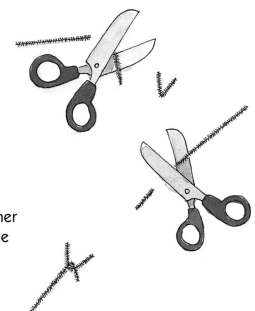

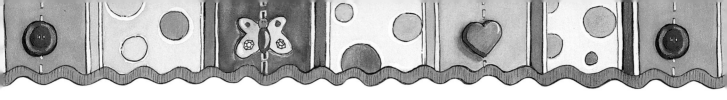

4. Cut the neck off a balloon. Cut a tiny slit in the top of the balloon.

5. Thread the bottom of the stem through the slit in the top of the balloon and out the opening at the bottom.

6. Pull the balloon up around the stamen to form a flower. Repeat steps and make two more flowers.

7. Press the Styrofoam ball on a flat surface to flatten one side. Glue the flattened side inside the clay pot.

8. Cut the neck off another balloon. Use the round part of the balloon to cover the pot or container.

(continued on next page)

9. Tie a pretty ribbon around the outside of the pot.

10. Trim the stems of the flowers so that the flower heads just peek over the edge of the pot when they are stuck into the Styrofoam ball.

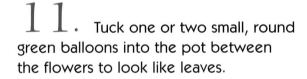

11. Tuck one or two small, round green balloons into the pot between the flowers to look like leaves.

The flower pot looks great sitting on an outdoor table. Or, try tying the three balloon flowers together, and pin them to a beach bag for a waterproof decoration.

Why use ordinary pushpins on a bulletin board when you can make these so easily?

Flower Pushpins

Here is what you need:

artificial flowers

stud earrings

white craft glue

Here is what you do:

1. Pull a flower apart so that the layers of petals are all separate.

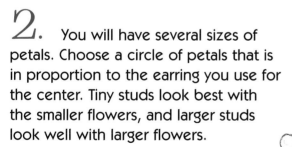

2. You will have several sizes of petals. Choose a circle of petals that is in proportion to the earring you use for the center. Tiny studs look best with the smaller flowers, and larger studs look well with larger flowers.

3. Push the stud through the center of the flower and secure it with glue.

The earring in the center of the flower makes a great pushpin for attaching messages to your bulletin board.

Each girlfriend will need to bring an old hand mirror to use for this project.

Magic Mirror Frame

Here is what you need:

photo of you

thin craft ribbon and trims

black pen

white paper

hand mirror

white craft glue

bottom part of a small box, such as a jewelry box

scissors

small flowers

Here is what you do:

1. Trim the photo to fit over the mirror. If the mirror is larger than the photo, cover the mirror with printed paper or fabric before attaching the photo.

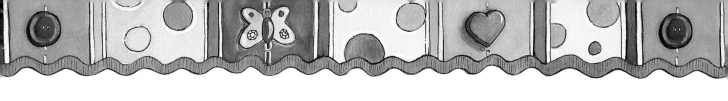

2. Glue the photo in place.

3. Glue trim around the photo.

4. Glue some tiny flowers around the photo and on the handle of the mirror.

5. Tie a piece of the thin ribbon in a bow around the handle.

6. Use the black pen to write "fairest of them all" on the white paper. Trim around the message and glue it to the handle of the mirror.

7. Glue the bottom of the box to the back of the mirror to serve as a stand for the frame.

**Don't let the wicked queen hear about you and your girlfriends!!
You know what happened to Snow White!**

Turn your favorite drop earrings into art with this project.

Earring Art Frame

Here is what you need:

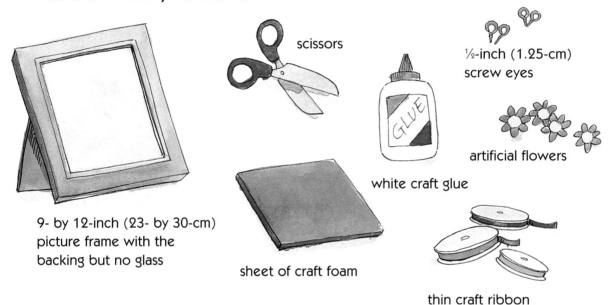

scissors

½-inch (1.25-cm) screw eyes

white craft glue

artificial flowers

9- by 12-inch (23- by 30-cm) picture frame with the backing but no glass

sheet of craft foam

thin craft ribbon

Here is what you do:

1. Place the craft foam in the frame as you would a picture. You may need to trim the edges a little to get a good fit.

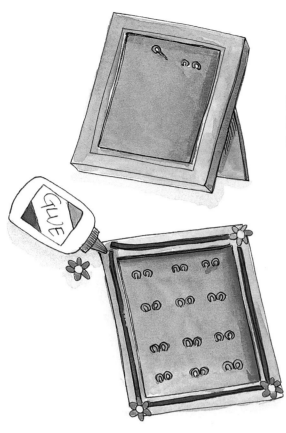

2. Put screw eyes into the foam to hang up pairs of earrings. You may want to hang up each pair of earrings as you put in the screws to help you with the spacing.

3. Glue a rim of thin ribbon to the frame and a ribbon bow at the top.

4. Glue an artificial flower in each corner of the frame.

Hang your earrings on the screw eyes to store them when not in use. They will make a very pretty display.

You and your girlfriends will make your doll friends
look very stylish with this craft idea.

Quick Doll Corsage

Here is what you need:

flower-shaped
shank button

pipe cleaner

white craft glue

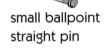
small ballpoint
straight pin

scissors

leaf-shaped
shank button

thin craft ribbon

Here is what you do:

1. Cut a 2-inch (5-cm) piece of
the pipe cleaner.

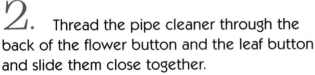

2. Thread the pipe cleaner through the
back of the flower button and the leaf button
and slide them close together.

3. Twist the ends of the pipe cleaner together to secure the two buttons.

4. Trim off any excess pipe cleaner, and fold the twisted ends to one side.

5. Make a tiny bow from the thin craft ribbon.

6. Glue the bow to the back of the corsage.

7. Use the ballpoint straight pin to attach the flower to the clothing of the lucky doll.

You can cut a small leaf from a larger leaf of an artificial flower if you do not have a leaf-shaped button.

Here is a quick and easy way to make a plain candle look exceptional.

Earring-Studded Candle

Here is what you need:

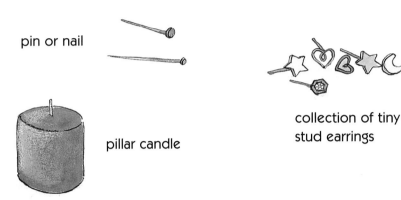

pin or nail

pillar candle

collection of tiny
stud earrings

Here is what you do:

1. Use the pin or nail to lightly scratch a simple shape on the side of the candle.

2. Cover the outline of the shape with tiny stud earrings. You can put them close together or leave some space between them.

Let friends and family know you are looking for discarded stud earrings and other jewelry, and you will have a box of crafting treasures in no time.

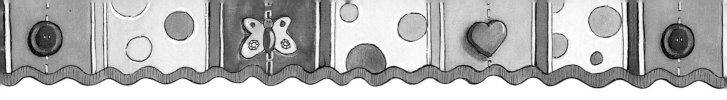

Everyone at the party can express herself with . . .

Wonderful Words

Here is what you need:

shape craft beads

sparkle stems

20-gauge wire

scissors

thin craft ribbon

ruler

Here is what you do:

1. Decide on a word that expresses something positive, such as giggle, laugh, love, friends, and joy. These are all good choices, but there are lots more.

2. Use the sparkle stems to write the word in cursive about 4 inches (10 cm) tall.

4"

(continued on next page)

3. Attach the sparkle stems to one another by twisting their ends together so that you have one stem long enough to make your word. As you form your word, whenever the stem goes across itself, wrap it all the way around itself to help secure each letter.

4. Use a shape bead at the top of any letter that requires a dot, such as the letter *i*.

5. Cut a piece of the wire twice as long as the word plus another 12 inches (30 cm).

6. Fold the wire in half. Weave the two ends of the wire in and out on each side of the bottom of the word. This will give it support and prevent the word from bending.

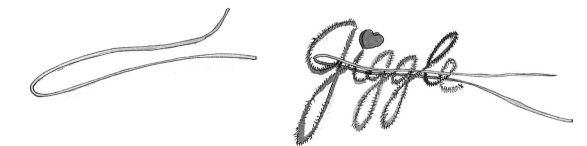

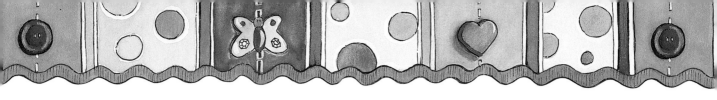

7. Twist the two ends of the wire together at the end of the word.

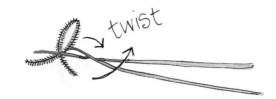

8. Slide some shape beads onto each excess wire end. Fold the end over the last bead on each wire to secure the beads.

9. Cut two 24-inch (60-cm) lengths of the ribbon.

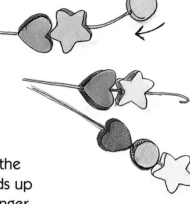

10. Thread a piece of ribbon through the letter at each end of the word. Bring the ends up and tie them together in a knot to make a hanger for the word.

Have your guests make surprise words for one another that reflect the personality of the receiver.

About the Author

Among the more than fifty craft books Kathy Ross has written are *Crafts for All Seasons, The Storytime Craft Book, All New Crafts for Valentine's Day, All New Crafts for Halloween, All New Crafts for Thanksgiving, All New Crafts for Kwanzaa,* and the earlier books in this series of books for girls, *Things to Make for Your Doll, All-Girl Crafts,* and *The Scrapbooker's Idea Book.*

For a complete list of Kathy Ross craft books, visit www.lernerbooks.com, or to find out more about the author, visit www.kathyross.com.